To: Jeanne
Merry Christmas)!
1995   Jackie

A Family in Liberia

LIBRARY OF CONGRESS CATALOGING-IN-PUBLICATION DATA

Humphrey, Sally.
   A family in Liberia.

   Summary: Describes the home, work, school, customs,
and amusements of ten-year-old Kamu and his family living
in the village of Mobuta in Liberia.
   1. Liberia—Social life and customs—Juvenile
literature. 2. Children—Liberia—Juvenile literature.
[1. Liberia—Social life and customs. 2. Family life—
Liberia] I. Title.
DT636.5.H85 1987   966.6'2   86-27229
ISBN 0-8225-1674-8 (lib. bdg.)

Manufactured in the United States of America

   2   3   4   5   6   7   8   9   10 97 96 95 94 93 92 91

A Family in Liberia

Sally Humphrey

Lerner Publications Company · Minneapolis

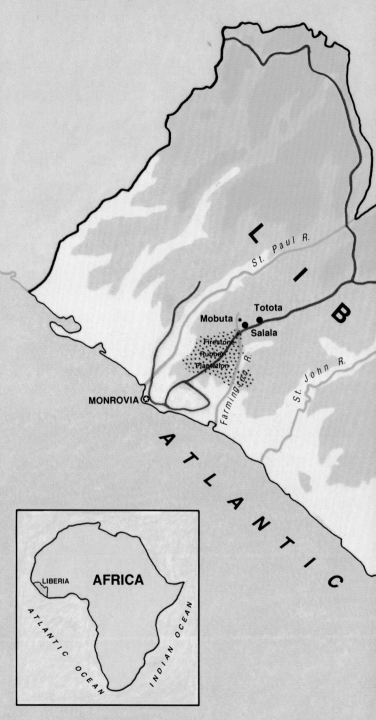

Kamu is ten years old. He lives in Mobuta (MOH-boo-tah) with his mother and father, his big sister Benu, his brother Baki, and his baby sister Massa.

Mobuta is a small village in the Salala (SAH-lah-lah) District of Liberia. It is a four mile (about 6 kilometer) walk to the nearest town, Salala. It takes one more hour by car to the capital, Monrovia.

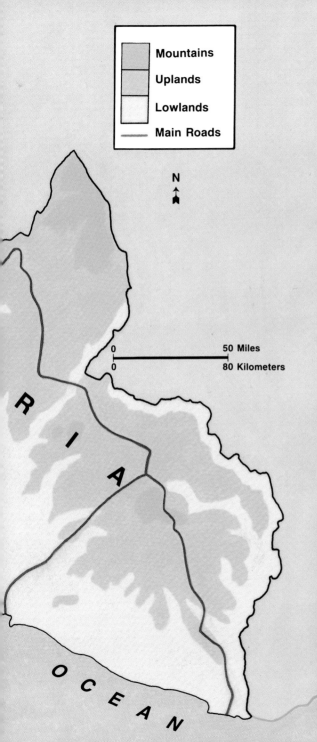

Mountains
Uplands
Lowlands
Main Roads

N

0   50 Miles
0   80 Kilometers

There are two families living in Mobuta—Kamu's family and his uncle's family. Kamu's father is the oldest man in Mobuta so he is the chief. He is a weaver, but he also has a rice farm just outside of Mobuta.

Kamu's family belongs to the Kpelle (PEH-lee) tribe, one of the largest tribes in Liberia. The Kpelle people live in the rain forest area of Liberia where the trees are very tall and thick and the rainfall is very high. There are over 16 tribes in Liberia, and all speak different languages. Kamu and his family speak a language called Kpelle. Liberian people learn to speak English as well as their own language so that they can talk with people from all the different tribes.

Today Kamu is bringing a large box of cloth to Mobuta from the market at Salala. His mother wants to make a dress for herself on her new sewing machine.

Kamu's father and uncle have planted fruit trees all around Mobuta. They have banana, orange, grapefruit, lime, mango, papaya, and oil palm trees. You can see the ragged leaves of the banana trees. Goats and chickens run around between the houses, but Kamu's family only eat meat on special occasions. With the fruit and vegetables growing around Mobuta and the rice farm outside the village, they grow almost all their own food.

There are twelve houses and a small shop in Mobuta. The ground between the houses is kept very clean to keep snakes away. Baki, Kamu's brother, loves to play with his cousins in the sand around the houses. When Kamu has to run errands for his mother, he sometimes wishes that he were still little like Baki. But when his mother thanks him for going to the market, he feels proud that he is old enough to help her.

Kamu's father has two wives. Kamu's mother is his first wife or head wife, so she is in charge of everything that happens in their home.

In the late afternoon, Kamu's mother has to think about getting dinner. Liberians eat rice with every meal. Kamu likes to help with the cooking and sometimes he cooks the rice with his cousin, Molley.

Molley crushes the rice in a wooden mortar. Then Kamu's aunt shakes the rice in her fanner. The heavy grains of rice stay in the flat fanner. The husks, which are lighter, blow away.

Kamu washes the rice in water and then cooks it in a black pot over the open fire.

Kamu's mother often makes palm butter soup with the red nuts that grow on the oil palm trees. First she goes to the stream to fetch a big pan of water. She boils the palm nuts until they are soft and then beats them in the mortar.

Benu and her cousins separate the hard seeds from the fibers and squeeze out the palm juice. Kamu's mother will cook the palm juice with a little chicken, some salt, and hot peppers or chilies.

When everything is ready, Kamu's mother calls the family around the fire. They all eat a big bowl of rice with the palm butter soup and tell each other the news from the day.

If Kamu's family grows more than enough fruit and vegetables for themselves, they sell some at the local market in Salala. Kamu's mother is on her way there with baby Massa tied to her back. She has a bucket full of mangoes to sell and a mat to sit on.

If she sells all her mangoes she will be able to buy something she cannot make or grow in Mobuta. Usually she must buy some kerosene for her lantern, but she has been saving her money and she would like to buy a radio. Kamu has wanted a radio for a long time so he can listen to the new songs that his friends always talk about.

The market is run mostly by women. On market day, everyone catches up on the latest news as well as buying and selling.

Almost everything a Liberian family needs can be found in the market. All of the foods Kamu's family grows are sold here. There are also tomatoes, onions, avocadoes, pineapples, peanuts, spices, and even medicines gathered from the forest. Foods like rice and palm oil are measured out in cups to be sold. Small animals like chickens and birds are kept in woven cages until they are sold.

At the end of the rainy season in October, Kamu's father chooses a new place in the forest for his rice farm. All the men and the oldest boys in Mobuta help cut down the trees and bushes on the new farm. When the wood is dry, they burn it. Kamu will help with the men's work when he is thirteen.

When the field is completely cleared, the women and children plant the rice seeds. Kamu's grandmother is the oldest woman in Mobuta, so it is her job to scatter the seeds evenly over the field. Then the younger women and the children use their short hoes to cover the seeds with soil.

Kamu helps plant the rice. When the sun beats down and blisters cover his hands, he wishes again that he was as young as Baki.

In May, the rainy season begins. The rice grows well in the warm, wet climate—it is about 80° F (27° C) all year long. While the rice is growing, Kamu, Baki, and all their cousins go to the farm every day. They must frighten away the birds and deer which would eat the rice.

When the rice is ripe, everyone in Mobuta goes to the farm to help cut it. Each stalk must be cut carefully with a small knife. The rice stalks are brought back into Mobuta. There the rice is dried and stored for the next year. It is important that Kamu's family grows enough rice to last the whole year, or they will not have enough to eat.

Kamu is lucky that his father and mother can afford to let him go to school. Many children cannot go to school because they are needed at home.

It is expensive to send Kamu to school. He must have a school uniform and he must buy his own books. This year Kamu's mother plans to make his uniform. His father sets aside some money each year especially for Kamu's books. Soon, textbooks may be supplied free by the government.

Kamu goes to the government school in Salala. He walks there and back every day. The school is a big building made of cement blocks. It has a corrugated iron roof. Every morning at 8:00 A.M. the children line up outside the school before they go into their classrooms.

The school holds classes for kindergarten through eighth grade. There are about 130 boys and 20 girls in the school.

Everything is taught in English. They study reading, writing, spelling, arithmetic, social studies, general science, and Liberian history. Kamu's favorite subject is Liberian history.

At 10:00 A.M. there is a fifteen-minute recess. Kamu always rushes outside with the boys to play soccer. The girls play hopscotch and jump rope.

At eleven-thirty, everyone gets a bowlful of cornmeal for lunch. This week it is Kamu's turn to help the cook.

School ends at one o'clock because it is too hot to work through the middle of the day.

Once a month, Kamu and the other boys bring their cutlasses to school. These long, wide knives are used to cut the grass on the soccer field. The girls bring their hoes to clear the weeds around the school building. The bare ground helps to keep snakes away from the school.

At the end of the school year in June, there is always a big soccer match against the neighboring town of Totota. Kamu was too young to be picked for the team this year, but he hopes to be goalkeeper next year.

Kamu and his friends climb into a tree to get the best view of the game. Kamu feels very proud of his team. They look sharp in their new uniforms.

When their team captain scores a goal in the first half, all the children clap and cheer. It is the only goal in the game, and the Salala team wins.

When Kamu is not in school or helping his mother or father, he likes to walk in the dark, cool forest with his brother Baki. The boys love to follow the paths through the tall trees and hanging vines.

In the forest they cannot see the sky at all. They are sure to hear birds screeching and see monkeys swinging from tree to tree. If they are very quiet, they may even see the red deer which live in the forest.

Sometimes they go as far as the Farmington River, where a special bridge has been made out of vines. This kind of bridge is always made in secret by the elders of the Kpelle tribe. The boys believe it is made by their gods.

Kamu and Baki love to feel the bridge sway back and forth as they walk across. They know they mustn't go too far on the other side of the river. They must always be home well before it gets dark or their mother and father will worry.

19

Kamu likes to watch his father weave. When he asks his father to teach him to weave, he always hears, "when you finish school." Kamu can hardly wait.

Each year, Kamu helps pick the balls of cotton and pull out the cotton seeds. His aunt makes the cotton fibers straight with two wire brushes. His grandmother spins the cotton into thread. Kamu helps his mother dye the thread and dry it in the sun.

Kamu's father made a loom out of sticks. He carefully lines up the threads on his loom. Then, sitting on one of the sticks, he starts to weave. Kamu watches and thinks about the time when he will be helping his father.

Kamu's father weaves long strips of cloth. He sews several long strips together to make blankets, long robes, and shirts. Mobuta is well known for its "country cloth." Country cloth is cloth woven by hand in the villages. People come from miles away to buy blankets and robes from Kamu's father.

Kamu's uncle wants a new house for his second wife, so he has asked Kamu and his cousins to build it. Kamu helps cut the sticks and palm leaves. Then the older boys make a frame of sticks for the walls and the roof. They tie all the sticks together with vines.

When they have finished the frame, Kamu helps them again. He mixes soil with water to make mud. His cousins push the mud between the sticks to make the walls. When the mud dries, they add more mud. They build up the mud until the walls are about six inches (15 centimeters) thick. Finally, they cover the walls with a layer of special clay to make them white.

One of the cousins uses the same method to build a small shed near the new house.

When the walls are finished, Kamu's cousins tie bunches of dried palm leaves to the roof. The rows of palm leaves overlap each other like shingles. Kamu's uncle watches closely to see that the boys are doing a good job. The roof must be thick enough to keep out the heavy rains in the rainy season and the hot sun in the dry season.

The inside of the house will be cool and clean. Kamu's aunt will pound the clay floor until it is firm, and once a week she will spread a new layer of mud over the floor to keep it smooth and tidy.

Saku, Kamu's oldest cousin, has finished school this year. He wants to go to the capital city, Monrovia, to try to find a job with an uncle. He doesn't want to be a farmer like his father.

Kamu has always wanted to see Monrovia. Saku has agreed to take him, since it is school vacation.

Kamu is very excited. He and Saku walk to the main road at Salala. They can wait there for a taxi to take them into Monrovia.

On the way to Monrovia, Kamu sees the forest of rubber trees at the huge Firestone Rubber Plantation for the first time. The Firestone Rubber Company built the road from Monrovia to the plantation in the 1920s. It also built schools and clinics for the workers. Several of Kamu's cousins want to go to work on the plantation.

Finally, the taxi comes into Monrovia. Kamu is amazed to see the wide streets lined with beautiful trees and filled with cars and buses.

Kamu and Saku will stay with their uncle, who lives in the large three-story house on the right. Their uncle is the manager of a small shoe factory. He will teach Saku how to use the machines in the factory. If Saku does well with his training, his uncle has promised him a job in the factory.

Saku is lucky his uncle lives in Monrovia. Many people who come to Monrovia to look for work have no place to live and cannot find a job.

Kamu has never seen sidewalks so crowded with people, or so many shops and stores. It is fun to drive by the hotels, restaurants, schools, and movie theaters that he has always heard about.

After a week in Monrovia, Kamu must go back to Mobuta. He will miss the noise and excitement of Monrovia, but he will be able to visit Saku again. Kamu still wants most of all to learn how to weave like his father in Mobuta.

History of Liberia

Liberia was formed in 1822 by freed American slaves who wanted a place to live in Africa. The freed slaves, called Americo-Liberians, settled mostly in cities along the coast. They declared the Republic of Liberia in 1847.

The Americo-Liberians built a country among the peoples who already lived in the area, like the Kpelle. They patterned the Liberian constitution and government after that of the United States. The Americo-Liberians were only a small number of the people who lived in Liberia. They made the laws and collected the taxes. Most native Liberians, however, were not allowed to vote.

At first, there were no roads or schools in the country. Rural people like Kamu lived very differently from the Liberians in the cities.

William Tubman, Liberia's president from 1944 to 1971, helped change things for rural Liberians. While he was president, public schools, clinics, and roads were built. Iron mines opened and offered more jobs.

Political strife and military takeovers mark Liberia's more recent history. William Tolbert, who became president after William Tubman, was killed in 1980 when Samuel Doe, an army sergeant, took over the government and named himself president.

Doe was the country's first president to be a native Liberian rather than an Americo-Liberian. He was formally elected in 1985 in the first national election in which all adults, not just wealthy landowners, were allowed to vote.

In 1990, civil war erupted. Two rebel groups, both led by ex-army leaders, killed President Doe as well as many civilians in Monrovia. After 14 months of bitter fighting, a West African peace-keeping force intervened to impose a cease-fire and install an interim government.

Facts about Liberia

Capital: Monrovia

Monrovia was named after United States President James Monroe. He helped the freed slaves who founded Liberia to settle in Africa.

Official Language: English

Each tribe speaks its own language, and two of the tribes read and write their tribal language. However, English is the language which unites the Liberians and which is used in government and business.

Form of Money: Liberian dollar

Area: about 43,000 square miles
(111,400 square kilometers)

Liberia is about the size of Tennessee.

Population: about 2 million people

About five percent of the population is descended from freed American slaves.

NORTH
AMERICA

SOUTH
AMERICA

EUROPE

A S I A

AFRICA

Liberia

AUSTRALIA

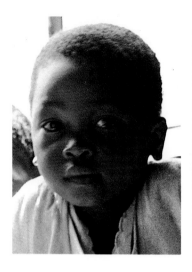

Families the World Over

Some children in foreign countries live like you do. Others live very differently. In these books, you can meet children from all over the world. You'll learn about their games and schools, their families and friends, and what it's like to grow up in a faraway land.

An Aboriginal Family	A Family in Hong Kong	A Family in Nigeria
An Arab Family	A Family in Hungary	A Family in Norway
A Family in Australia	A Family in India	A Family in Pakistan
A Family in Bolivia	A Family in Ireland	A Family in Peru
A Family in Brazil	A Kibbutz in Israel	A Family in Singapore
A Family in Chile	A Family in Italy	A Family in South Korea
A Family in China	A Family in Jamaica	A Family in Sri Lanka
A Family in Egypt	A Family in Japan	A Family in Sudan
A Family in England	A Family in Kenya	A Family in Taiwan
An Eskimo Family	A Family in Liberia	A Family in Thailand
A Family in France	A Family in Mexico	A Family in West Germany
	A Family in Morocco	A Zulu Family

Lerner Publications Company, 241 First Avenue North, Minneapolis, Minnesota 55401